Sun and Sky
Poetry and art by Kindred

For my sun and sky, my moon and stars.

Table of Contents

i. The Heart (the love stuff)
ii. The Little things (quotes and micro)
iii. The Others (misc.)

The Heart

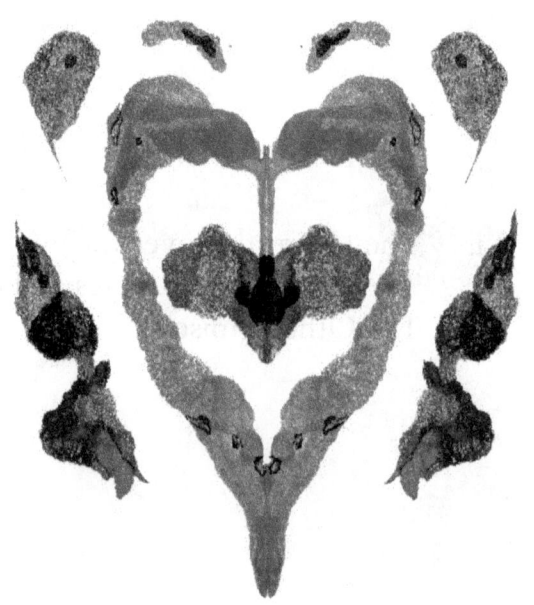

A Bloom Amid Chaos

A path to singularity,
a doe left in a trance.
She does not ease her head to see,
nor twitch from nature's dance.

She simply holds her gaze on end
amid the angry storm.
Fierce thunder claps, but does not break
her unrelenting form.

A vision bold holds sway on her
and in the distance, looms.
A bristling mate with antlers wide
stands tall amongst the booms.

She gives no care to dangers near
nor heeds approaching night,
for set upon her swelling heart
is love in all its might.

To Live Without Love

To live without love
is to walk beyond peace.
The battles within
will erupt without cease.

A hollow existence
will forever endure,
benighted of the ardor
of fairytales and lore.

To live without love
is to wallow in scorn.
But to live without your love
is to linger forlorn.

Patience

She was my destiny
ages before there was such a thing.
Before the Babylonians
spilled blood on holy soil -
before the Nasca lines were scratched into parched earth -
before the Sumerians carved
thoughts onto stone tablets -
before the first eyes
gazed at a blazing night sky
and pondered ancient mysteries,
and before that same sky
exploded with a miraculous
shower of heat and light -
our paths were already crossed.
It was already so.

Destiny is the profit of patience.

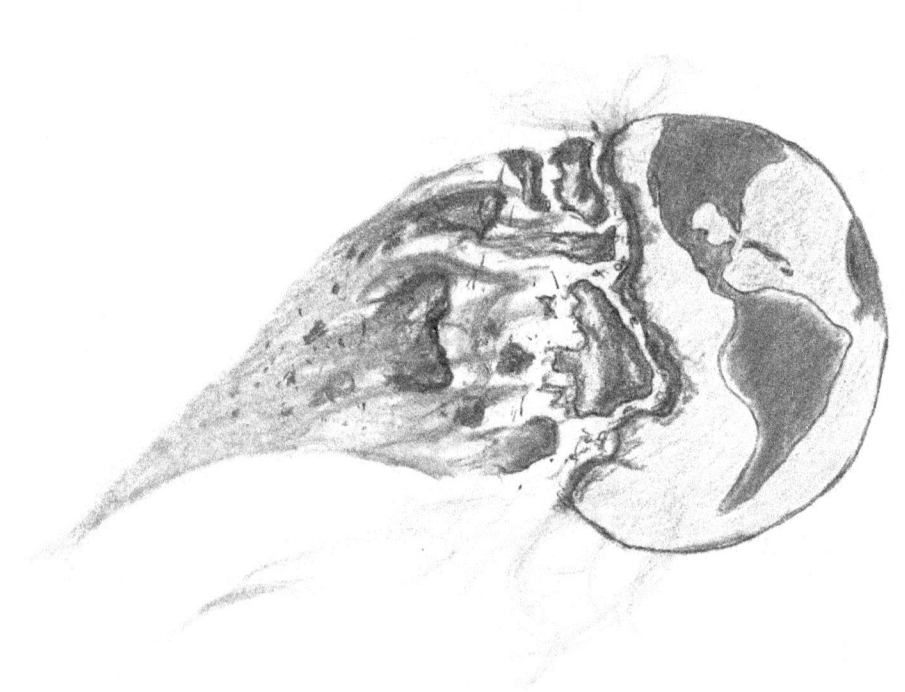

A Fateful Day

Some fateful day
I will breathe no more.
The memory of my name
will fade from the earth
as quickly as my lungs deflate.
My flesh will become fodder
for the miniscule.
My bones will slowly crumble
and turn to dust.

All of this world will suffer
a similar end.

Leaders will rise and fall.
Towers will topple.
Civilizations will transition
to footnotes in a history book -
those, too, will disintegrate with time.

Some fateful day
all that will remain
of this glorious universe
is darkness, bitter cold,
and my love for you.

Mere Kids

Mere kids were we
when first we met long ago -
yet to be blemished by love,
naive to the impacts of change.

Young are we still
in the depths of ourselves
each time we touch.
We relive gentle moments,
soft spoken promises,
and whispers of tomorrow.

Mere kids were we
and forever shall be.

All That She Is

She is the vibrant color
that graces a blank canvas.

An epiphany
that wakes me at 2 a.m.

A spark of focus
illuminating the fog.

She is a five-leaf clover
in a field of three.

The blooming foxglove
on the edge of a barren meadow.

A deep red rose
in a landscape of frozen white

and a lush garden
in the bleakest desert.

She is a lone sunbeam
piercing swollen clouds.

A burst of lightning
bound by no storm.

A supernova
in a sky of infinite black.

She is an orchestra
among silent fools.

The perfect notes
forming exquisite sheet music.

A symphony
amid white noise.

She is a Goddess
on Earth,

surrounded by mortals
longing to submit
to her every whim.

Immortalized

Let me immortalize you
with my ink;
present you to a world
unaware of your splendor.

Allow me to fill the pages
with lines of your triumphs,
tales of your glory,
and rhymes of your beauty.

For too long have they
been kept ignorant
to the power of your grace.
Let me captivate the masses
so that they, too,
shall bow to your presence.

Amazing Grace

She is a holy space,
salvation's embrace,
my amazing grace.

She is my carnal sin,
teasing angel skin,
salvation lies within.

She is my confession,
satan's repression,
my idol obsession.

She is my heaven's gate,
that true sacred place,
my coveted fate,
my amazing grace.

Before I Find You

If you find love
before I find you
promise me you'll embrace it.

If I reach out
in the harsh realness of life -
if I reach out too late,
promise to turn away from me.

If you find solace
in the solid form of another
before I find you,
say you'll not let go

and not look back.

I will love you with all I have
come heaven or hell
no matter the distance
no matter the years

but if you grow tired
and I remain in this digital prison
don't give up on hope.

Find it wherever you are,
in all that you do.

Promise to embrace it
the way that I hold you
each time I close my eyes.

Say you'll embrace it
if you find love
before I find you.

Before

Before, there was nothing.
Not even emptiness.
With no forms to be filled
the idea of emptiness had yet to be born.

There was no flesh and blood,
good nor evil,
sinner nor saint.

Nor did even silence exist.
There was never a sound,
and absent of sound
there is no concept of silence.

Before, there was no fire to forge,
no molecules to clump;
no matter existed, dark or other.
No light would glimmer
in the nothingness
that was neither vast
nor miniscule.

Before, there was no time,
no life and no death.
There was nothing,
but there was still "us".

Find in Me

Find in me
the light you need,
I will glow the darkest days.

Look to me
when you are lost
in this mindless, numbing maze.

Take from me
the breathe you seek
when your lungs are failing you.

Learn from me
forgotten words,
I can teach them all anew.

Follow me
into my dreams,
you will see where you have been.

Find in me
the love you crave,
I will help you feel again.

For Every Action

When you breathe,
I breathe.
You smile,
I shine.
You laugh
and I live.

But if you stumble,
I fall.
If you lose,
I fail.
You cry
and I shatter.
You hurt
and I bleed.
You bleed,
I scar.
And if you die
I die, too.

In Your Dreams

I do not simply
want to be *in* your dreams,
I want to *be* your dreams.

Your present and now.
Your tomorrow and future.
Your dreams in life
and beyond death.

But I do not simply
want to *be* your dreams,
I want us to create dreams
together.

Clovers

I want to watch you
hunt for clovers
in a field that we maintain.

I want to hold you
as we gaze at stars
in our sky, without refrain

And then kiss sweetly
as clouds encroach
and the minutes slowly wane.

I want us to dance
to a symphony
played quietly by the rain.

I want to slumber
within the warmth
your body cannot restrain

and soon awaken
to your gracious lips
as you mark me with their stain.

I want us to have
the kind of love
even time cannot contain.

I want to watch you
hunt for clovers
in a field that we maintain.

Just Like That

Like a storm loves the wind
and a river loves a stream.
How day kisses night
on the doorstep of a dream.

The way that thunder follows a bolt
as it cracks a bleeding sky.
The way that lovers breathe in step
as they touch, burn, and sigh.

Like this rain cleansing my soul.
Like the part that longs to be whole.

Yeah, just like that.

Left Behind

All of my kindness
leads me to blindness.
All of my silence
leads me to violence..

..just the same.

All of my shame
is left behind
for you to find.

And all of my pain
will still remain
long after your mind..
..has left me behind.

She and the Sea

She,
the tempestuous sea.
I,
the capsizing vessel.

She makes of me sunken wreckage

And I could drown a thousand times
and a thousand times
I would sail again.

Light

My luminous lighthouse
on dancing display.
The light in my lantern
igniting my way.

My radiant rhapsody,
so beguilingly bright.
My glimmering goddess
of infinite starlight.

Madness

In my madness I kissed you.
I grabbed your hand,
caressed your cheek
and kissed you deep.
Like an ocean of passion
released into a river of regret.
In my madness
I kissed you
and in your madness
you kissed me back.
Deep enough to drown my longing.
Strong enough to bind my sorrow.

We shared a gaze,
we shared our kiss,
then I opened my watering eyes

and you were gone.

Mind Meld

I need you to understand
that you are always on my mind.
From the moment my eyes open
until they close again in twilight,
and surely in between.
When not at the forefront,
you are tucked away
in the deep recesses of my subconscious,
but still always there.
An unintentional mind-meld
has left me this way..
and I would not change a thing.

Moments Within the Spaces

I taste your innocence so sweet
and drink from the chalice
that is your perfection.
I savor the succulent nectar
and I am alive again.

On fire I fall,
face in the dirt,
but rise from the ashes
upon taking your hand.
Like a phoenix,
I rise renewed.

I fall and yet I rise;
die and yet I live.
I cry, though filled with joy,
and choke with bruised lungs
until you give the air that parts my lips.

With a mere whisper
you give meaning to the undefined,
revealing long secluded answers
to questions on life and love and purpose.

But without you
I am parched and desolate.
A shriveling vessel,
hollow, if not for the dusty remains
of your memory.

Lend me but a moment of your brilliance
and I am fulfilled unto the dusk of my journey.
Simply offer me your precious time
and I will live forever within it.

Moonshine

Until night bestows moonshine
upon the magically starved
I will wander hopeless.
I will wander empty.

Until morning gives light
to a suffering horizon
I will lie awake.
I will lie wasted.

But when your light glints
upon the budding morn
I can be born anew
and bask in the warmth of your blaze.

And when your moonshine flows
into the shadows of my weary gloom
I will lay with wide eyes no more
and rest in the aftermath of your glow.

Musings (or Nothing, Everything)

A mirror.
A windowpane.
My present
and future fane.

Like a song I've never heard,
yet still know every word.

We are everything,
but we are tragic.
We are nothing,
but we are magic.

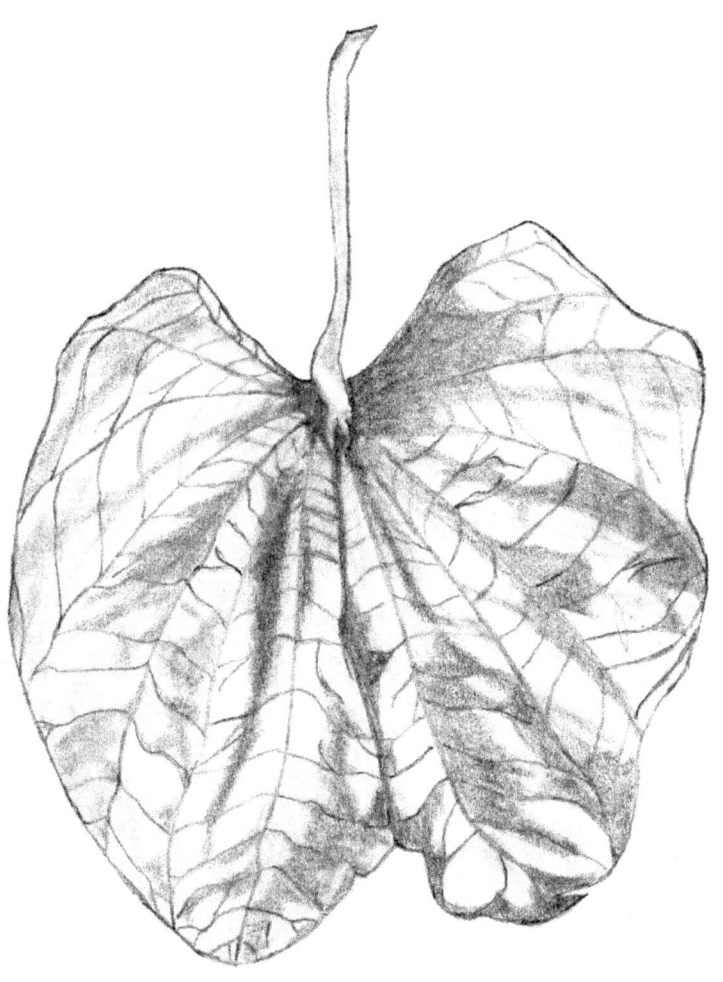

Sproutling

We planted a seed
just below the surface.
From this seed
sprung a sproutling.
Its roots grew deeper everyday,
ensuring not even the strongest wind
nor deepest flood
could rip it asunder.
Soon, with fathomless roots anchored far,
this sproutling scaled the sky
like the Tower of Babel.
Blossoms popped here and there,
dotting its endless limbs
with vibrant color.
Higher and higher it ascended
until it pierced the clouds.
Finally, absent of the limitations
imposed by the world,
this ever-growing Hawthorn
was granted the space
to flourish eternally.

Catalyst

As the sun descends
to embrace a pining horizon
and the moon aspires
to illuminate a sullied sky

you are there -

behind each inciting dream
on the brink of fruition
and every hope
of fantasy fulfilled.

You are the ignition
of unbridled ecstasy
and the remains
of desire realized.

You are the source
and substance of epiphany
and the method
within creation's madness.

You are the true catalyst
for the swooning heavens -

why the moon dreams
and the sun radiates.

Parachute (Roller Coaster)

I didn't fall slowly,
it was a rapid descent.
That feeling you get
in the pit of your stomach
on a roller coaster kind of fall.

I will continue to fall everyday
and never need a parachute
and never hit the ground.

Sculptor, Savior

My threads fall to the floor -
I am undone.
With scars on display,
my disguise unraveled,
I come to you.
I am humbled and broken,
bare and unfurled.
Let your breath be the wind
that gathers my scattered pieces
like monarchs in a net.
For I am a multitude of busted clay
longing for reformation.
And you are the artist,
merciful and generous,
with skilled hands for reshaping.

Sculptress

Like a sculptor, you are molding me
piece by piece into a better man.

Dust and debris settle in the aftermath
of your precise strikes.
I can feel my rough edges
begin to give way to new form below,
their structural integrity compromised.
My exoskeleton slowly cracks and splinters.
This artificial chrysalis falls away,
now frail and useless,
as you direct your blows.
I will emerge vulnerable,
but evolved,
waiting for your next swing.

She

She is a coded language
yet to be deciphered -
fascinating and mysterious.

She is a lost gospel -
the missing chapter
of an unfinished epic.

She is the knowledge
I strive to learn,
the memory
I would die to make,
and the unrelenting desire
I cannot quench.

She is my universal truth,
my waking motivation,
and the crux I long to unravel.

I am blissfully lost in the enigma
that is 'she'.

Someone, You

Something old,
something new.
Something borrowed,
something blue.

Somehow fell,
somehow flew.
Somehow loved,
somehow, you.

Someone warm,
someone true.
Someone loved,
someone, you.

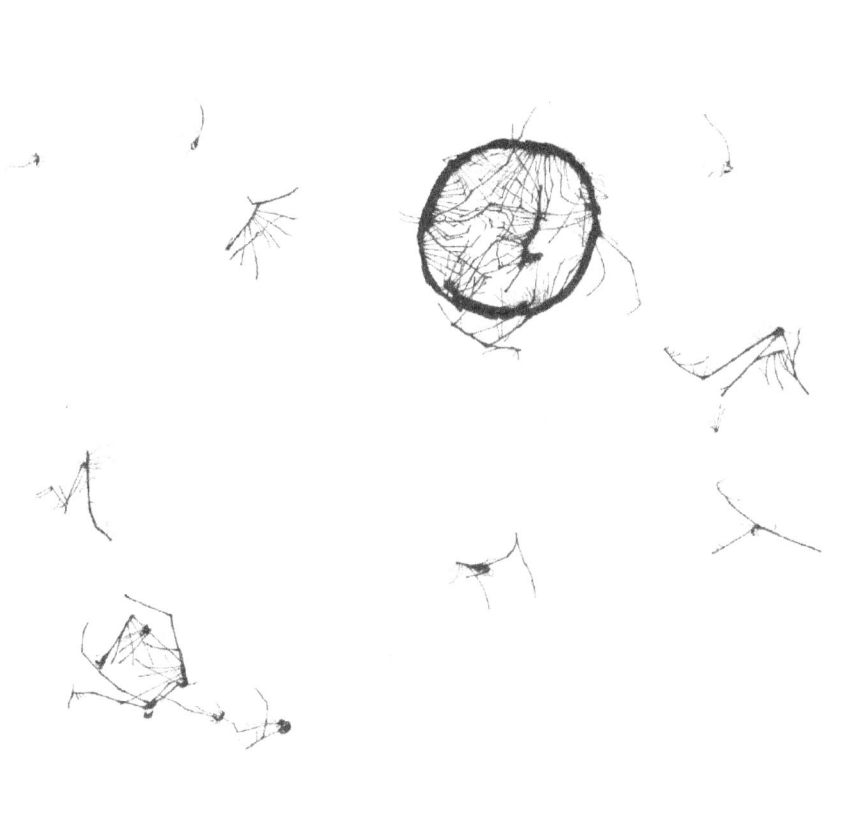

Strange Things in Love and Gravity

There is a fierce connection building between us.
No, not building.
It is being unearthed
like an ancient and glorious relic of another lifetime.
It has always existed
woven somewhere deep
within the fabric of time itself.
There, it is safe
and free to grow everlasting.
Promised by fate to never wane,
to never subside.
Only to evolve into something brighter
and more splendid with each passing eon.
The push of your gravity
warps time and space,
rivaling the super massive;
it draws me closer to your center.
A force like dark matter,
unseen, but felt throughout
in everything I do.
I am spun in your cosmic vortex.
Outward force fusing our bodies
like melted glass.
We will spin and sway lockstep,
entwined for eternity
like crystalline dancers.
Ours, an ethereal love story
born of stardust,
keeping pace with the universe.
A love story that will outlast time itself.

The Hurricane

She is the calm center of a hurricane
and the glorious chaos that surrounds it,
all at once.

Beautiful and dangerous.
Innocence wrapped in heavenly arousal.

An irresistible collision
of everything I need, want, and yearn to touch.

She is a swirling cataclysm
of lustful longing,
enduring passion,
and unconditional love.

She is a soothing rain.
She is a gentle breeze.
She is a hurricane.

The Light

I dreamt of you
in all your splendor
and all your strength.
You were jousting demons
with grace and courage.
You faced down evil
as it wielded its facade
as a weapon.

I dreamt of you
overcoming life
and all its obstacles.
Conquering a gauntlet
of lies, bruises, and monsters.

You shined so intensely,
the shadows were effaced.
The terrors had nowhere to hide
and the demons cowered
back into the nether.

I dreamt of you
being you
and growing stronger
in the face of turmoil,
emerging unblemished.

The Painter and the Poet

You are the palette,
full of endlessly gorgeous possibilities.
I am merely the brush,
humbly trying to find the right mix.

You are the ink,
writing your soul into cosmic fabric.
I am but an empty pen,
wishing to encapsulate your magic.

The Title is 'You'

If I were to write a poem
it would be about you.
Everything that you are,
everything you are not
and everything that you do.

It would be triumphantly profound,
and stretch far beyond the breach.
It would be perfectly flawed,
enthralling, and deep as an abyss,
yet pale beside the depth of your reach.

If I were a writer,
not some pathetic withering form,
maybe then I could pay tribute
to the magnitude of your impact
as it swells and sweeps me like a storm.

I would scribe about feats never seen -
unheard of tales of marvels and might.
Like the majesty of your song,
the breadth of your luminous voice
and how it glows amid the bleakest night.

If I were a poet
I would pen you into my story.
But alas, I am but a man
captivated by your glory.

Time and Torment

Time is an illusion.
It is a construct
of intelligent consciousness.
It does not exist beyond the plane
of sentient thought -
then why do I hear
each tick of the clock
like a heart beat in my ear?
How can it be
that I continue to choke
on the loss of something
that never was?
Why does every second
that you are away from me
feel like a spear between my ribs?
If time does not exist,
then how does it torture me so?

Unfiltered

She is beauty unfiltered,
unbridled and unblemished.
Her allure goes deeper than bone
and further than the supple flesh
that binds it all together.

Her splendor comes from
a life of tribulation
and challenges,
and from conquering them all.

It comes from a life spent
making life for others
worth living.

Her beauty is not just
the kind that incites jealousy
within the heart of Aphrodite;
it is much more than that.

Hers is a selfless glow
that knows no limitations.
It is spawned from
a boundless love
and she shares it willingly,
even with a bruised soul
as undeserving as mine.

Hers is a fresh kind of beauty,
new and redefining,
yet timeless and battle proven.

She requires no mask.
She needs no filter.

Yesterday, Tomorrow

You,
The spark of thought in every line.
The dark within I can't decline.
The epiphany that floods the page.
A luminous glow upon the stage.

The tempting muse that bleeds my pen;
the ink that always fills it again.
The fuel for creation in silent times
sparking visions of future rhymes.

You,
The Zen of my spirit
through chaotic seas.
That feeling of peace
traveling the breeze.

The scent of yesteryear
that ignites my mind
and the memory of tomorrow
that I strive to find.

You,
the healer of all sorrow;
now, yesterday, tomorrow.

You Are Not My Moon

You are not merely my moon,
full and luminous in the night sky.
Nor my sultry sun,
blazing for eternity.
And you are not my scattered stars,
guiding me along this journey.

You are more.

You are my wind -
the driving force upon my back
when I feel like giving in.

You are my Aurora -
a vibrant, flowing display of wonder.
Colorful and mysterious,
inciting a riot of creation in my soul.

You are my shimmering shores
of Vaadhoo,
spilling your iridescent glow
along my edges.

You are the sky -
a gentle place for Heaven to rest,
and you are the gravity
binding it all together.

You are not my moon and stars,
nor my sun and sky..

You are so much more.

Wild, Wonderful, and Wicked

I can feel this monster inside of me,
it is dying to get out.
Twisting my bones,
pushing up through my skin.
Its touch is searing
as it scratches beneath my flesh.
This beast aches to be released
so desperately that it may very well
destroy its vessel from inside out.
A new creature will be revealed
in our stead;
something stronger, brighter, bolder.
Something pure and brilliant,
yet wicked.
Like the point where heaven
kisses hell,
or the gentle fire that combusts
from the merging of angel and demon.
A love poised
to be wild, wonderful,
and wicked.

This love is like a caged beast
that must grow wild and untamed.
And I am bursting at the seams.

The Little Things
(quotes, haiku, and other micropoetry)

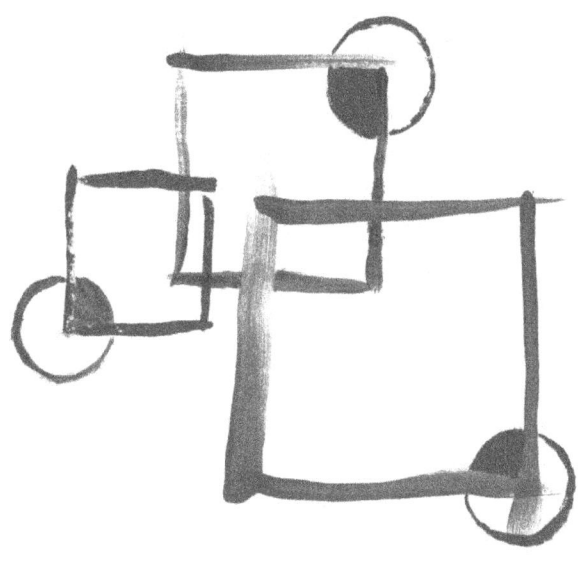

Weathered String Bracelet

Weathered string bracelet
loosely resting on my wrist -
thoughts of serendipity.

Upcycling

There is beauty in death,
if only in the hopes
of peace and rebirth
and their confluence
within nature.

Under the Influence

You affect me dramatically.
I can feel it
in everything that I do,
in every word that I write.

These Quiet Walls

It is so lonely in this room
without you;
only the walls whisper to me.
They ask me where you've gone.

Sun and Sky

You and I
bound forever
like sun and sky

Stirred

To stir her emotions,
that is my purpose.
Until she has spent
and has felt all that exist.
Only then
can she truly know me,
and I, her.

Stardust

My love was born
of stardust
and to stardust
it shall return.

Song from the Voiceless

You are like a song from the voiceless -
beautiful, majestic, powerful, and refined.

Single Star

I don't need
the whole universe;
a single star is enough.

Puzzle

You are the total of all your parts,
whether they fit together or not.
And I love each and every
wonderfully flawed
and beautiful piece.

Perfection

I would never venture to fix you.
One cannot fix perfection.

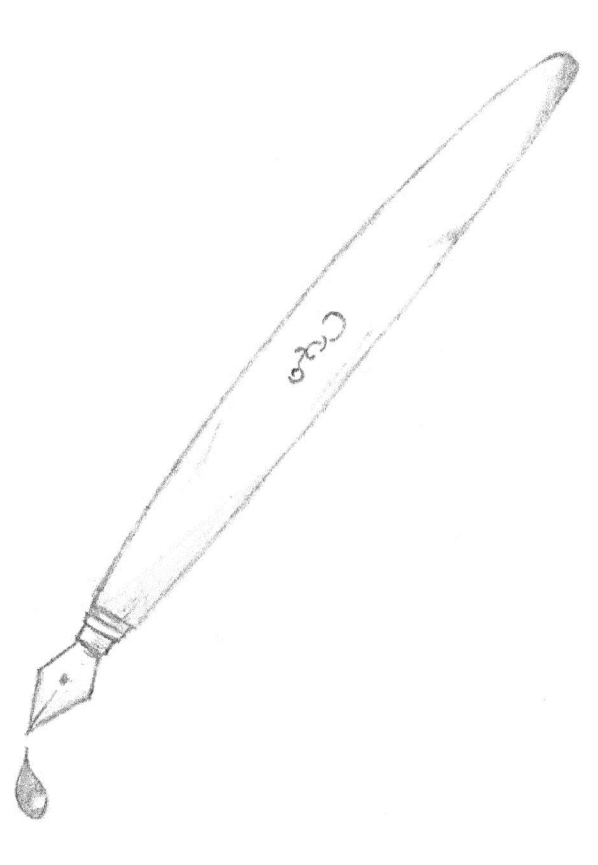

A Fleeting Thing (Heroic Quatrain)

Sweet muse, you must push my pen on this night.
Do not presume to be as morning dew,
for that shall disappear in the sunlight
and leave me wanting for more drops of you.

Eyes of Destiny

My destiny was not written in the stars -
    it was there all along,
        painted in your eyes.

Parallel Universe

Somewhere, there is a parallel
universe with a different you
and a different me.
They are in love, too.

Of Gravity, Light, and Darkness

How long can I keep her gravity at bay?
Soon, she will command all the light
this universe has to give

and I will be left in the dark.

My Flame

Until my flame
is extinguished
I will write
for you.

More than a Memory

I know that we were meant to be
more than just a memory,
more than just a dying glimpse
of a love that used to be.

Broken Pen

Without you, I would be fractured.
Broken from my heart
all the way through my pen.
This heart would never again beat
and this pen would never again bleed.

Magic

I believe in magic
because I see it in you
every day.

This magic I see in you,
in turn,
breathes through me.

Mad Love

No matter what the future brings
know that I loved you in this moment
with more madness and fervor
than I ever thought possible.

Lonely Echo

My words pierce the hollow
and echo forlorn.

Like a Storm

Touch like rain,
kiss like thunder,
sigh like wind.

Love like the storm
that rages within.

In Darkness, a Light

I Dream in Time

Sometimes, when I close my eyes,
all I see is my future.

All I see is you.

There is no past.
There is no present.
There exists only this dream.

Hushed Heart

Do not surrender your
lovely heart to anyone else.
Keep it secret.
Keep it safe for me.

Holy Trinity

She is my holy trinity -
beauty, soul, and mind.

From Rubble

I crumbled like cinders
and crashed upon the floor.
You gathered the rubble
and rebuilt me, once more.

Ashton

Her suffering expunged;
soul set free into Elysium.

Collide

Hearts pound
as we finally collide.
Stardust consumes
the rubble
of wasted years.

Burn

Your impact spreads like wildfire
and I am but the helpless weeds.

Let it burn.

Success -
Putting everything you have
into everything you do.

Poetry should be free
of the chains than bind us,
body and mind,
and yet
seep with the emotions
those chains create.

If you quit now,
how will you ever
rub it in their faces?

It is often not as impressive
to hold on
as it is to let go.

My greatest fear is simply to be afraid
and in turn, be crippled by it.

Go boldly into that
dark beyond
for that is the path
to discovery,
that is the way to growth.

You must walk with fire at your feet
to not know the coldness of retreat.

Evolution is the conduit
to survival.
What better time than now
for us to evolve?

When you're ready to cross that bridge
you won't have to cross it alone.

*You cannot truly
appreciate victory
without first
knowing defeat.*

Challenge is the fuel of the strong
and the fear of the weak.

Fading Scars

Aching wounds will heal.
Remnants of scars dissipate.
Skin reborn to feel.

Ghosts that Never Were

Nefarious ache,
a longing like vellichor.
Hiraeth beckoning.

In the Wind

You set me adrift,
lost like an aimless vessel.
You were my anchor.

A Lighted Night as the World Closes its Eyes

Do not dread the night.
Truth be told,
darkness fears your light.

Shadows Linger

Speak to me gently
foul shadow of yesterdays.
Your visage is bleak.

The Others

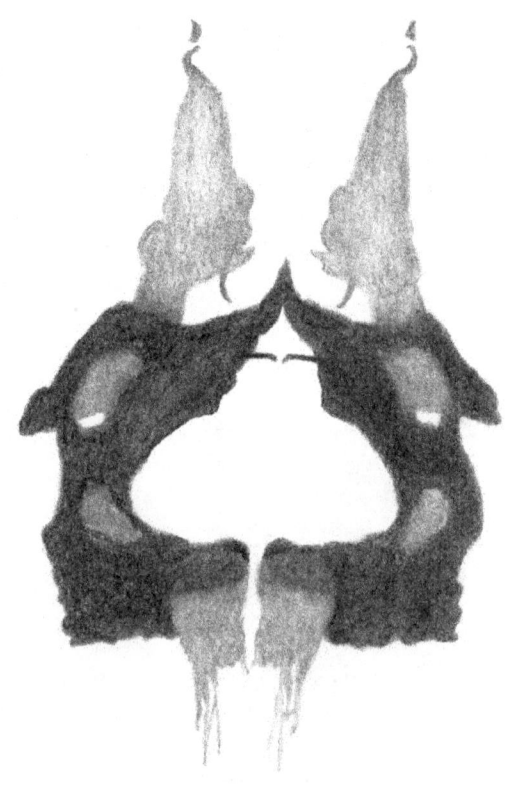

Night Canvas

The moon radiates
from the stolen light
of another.
A desperate facade,
but the ultimate compliment -
striving, for eternity,
to mimic such pure light.

Burning conglomerates of molecules
dot an infinite black canvas
surrounding our mockingbird moon.
It is abstract art
even the masters have envied.

A Glimmer in the Creator's Eye

Perhaps this universe is the mind of our "creator"
and we are but the thoughts and dreams within it.

Perhaps our universe is one of many in a vast multi-verse
because our God is one of many beings
living, thinking, and dreaming in a realm of many.

Perhaps this universe seems to be expanding
because the mind of our God grows as he or she learns.

Perhaps the big bang that birthed our universe
was simply the mind of our God sparking to life upon his own birth.

Perhaps we are all just an elaborate figment
of His imagination.

No Vacancy

Beneath the gaze of the wretched
find me there, fetal,
searing under their blank stare.

I crane to face the burden
of my endlessly troubled selves,
but find no redemption there.

Solace makes no home
in a mind cluttered and seeping.
Even the spiders are claustrophobic within.

So lock the door as you go
and leave me with the whispers,
lest you too be consumed by sanity's sin.

Breath of Mankind

We built our history upon stone
and the shoulders of our ancestors.
We etched it onto ancient walls
and ancient souls
which carry the legacy onward.

But the era of mankind
began with the softest of things -
a breath.

That single whisper of precious life
demolished the barriers of evolution.
That simple, catalystic breath
spawned pillars, temples, and cities -
invention, growth, and empires -
war, destruction, and ruins.

This fragile blink of existence
carries with it the power
to shape our world

or to destroy it.

Balance

The breadth of my ambition
is yet unknown.
It pines and it burns
and respects
no boundaries.
It grows in its longing
for fealty,
and accepts no less
than personal apex.

And depth of my tholance
is yet untested.
Strike me with lash,
bind me with chain -
I will not rescind.
Struggle breeds revelation.

A balance between vision
and tolerance of defeat
must be achieved.

Ambition unchecked
is the path to despair.

Of Wickedness and Woe

Between shadow and twilight,
in the depths of your despair,
I linger.

In the malicrux of your past,
that piercing throe inside your chest
or the ache of loss in each breath,
I linger.

I am of wickedness
and I am of woe.
Loe to the weary traveler,
disillusioned from treacherous lengths,
who treads upon my path.

I am the chill down your spine,
the sweat that beads on your brow,
the elusive air that escapes your lips.

I am the swell of a wave
breaching the shore -
a tsunami cracking dry earth.

I am an unforeseen drought
upon your fertile lands
and the ensuing famine you feel
when emptiness squirms within.

I am the consuming pestilence
that besieges you.
The epic plague
that scholars of old
penned into journals.

I am the feat of will
that parts an angry sea,
and the perpetual force
that levels it back against you.

Fear my gaze,

for I am the trail you forge
with each fateful step
and I am the terminus
of every human odyssey.

Tremble at my name,
for I am born of wickedness.
I am the harbinger of woe.

Glass Ceiling

The heart of creativity
has no master.
It suffers no chains,
bears no weight,
and dwells not in a cage
with kings nor slaves.

The beauty of creation
cannot be bound
by tyrants
nor defined in books.
It is held only by
papier-mâché limits
we place on ourselves -
fragile boundaries
begging to be shattered.

Lilith

She is the one with black wings.
The one damnation brings,
for whom the devil sings.

Bore from the loins of earth,
but driven by primeval needs.
She kisses with split tongue
and performs lascivious deeds.

She roams where the wild ones are
and grazes on the hearts of men.
Mistress of the bleak and bizarre,
she slithers forth from evil's den.

Lilith, of soil and dust,
a creature of boundless lust,
betrayer of Adam's trust.

She is the one with black wings,
seducer of slaves and kings -
for Lilith, the devil sings.

Orange is the New White

We fall undramatically
like leaves after death,
pushed and pulled by unseen laws,
unceremoniously discarded and forgotten.
We the people,
the ones under orange tinted thumbs,
cascade down from walls
that will never be built.
We gather below their boots,
crumbled and decaying,
waiting for the wind
to scatter our remains
when all we really need to do

is UNITE.

Primitive Skies

Perhaps this is how
prehistoric man viewed the stars.
Heads tilted, eyes wide.
Primitive minds racing,
struggling to quell
the confusion,
overwhelmed by possibilities.
Searching for that one flicker
of understanding.
Just one glimmer
of meaning
in an endless sky
of questions.

Salt (or Sorrow Amongst Loathsome Tides)

Lost at sea,
in this abyss of tears
rung violently from ones being
like a rag compressed and twisted.

An empty bottle
bobs up and down
as waves pound the veneer;
it's been long stripped of its note.

Save me, it may have read.
Rescue me from this ocean of the lost.

Woe, instead it is empty,
but for the gulps of salty liquid
from its war with the laws of nature.

The doomed vessel
struggles to maintain buoyancy,
adrift in a self-made pool of nothingness.

It slowly drowns
under wave after wave
of unrelenting emotional tides.

Find no love
nor savior here.
Only salt water and remorse.

The Agony

The pain is my skin.
I wear it as my own.
Embrace it like a long lost lover.

I no longer know what I am,
nor who I am,
absent of the agony.

A pile of broken pieces
that refuse to fit together
without a hammer and sweat.

I am a trail of tears and blood
forging through a forest of thorns.
The light that breaks is not but anguish.

Set agony upon my crown,
I will lap up the metallic drops it spawns.
Suffering feeds my will to carry on.

The pain is my bones.
I feel it beneath my flesh,
stretching, snapping, writhing.

It is a welcome sensation.
Like the memory of a friend
seeping through from days beyond.

I let it cascade through me
as it does its work,
reminding me that I am alive

and I was built to endure.

Connect the Dots

I enjoy watching the stars
in the silence of twilight,
connecting the luminous dots
as though their design
will reveal the truth
of a grand mystery.
But there is no paradox
behind the stars.
They burn because they must.
And I revere them for that.
Like them,
I burn from within

because I must.

We All Sail to Our Own Ends

Every breath we take
is like wind swelling a sail,
pushing us ever closer
to an inevitable end.

For some,
that breath is a calm breeze.
For others,
each exhale is a typhoon.

String Theory

The answer to all is written
in the molecules of stars.
It is woven into the fabric
of the fields of Higgs.
It is vibrating
within the power
of the God particle,
invisible except to the few
who embrace it
and know the language.

It is more than a theory
of everything -
it is the solution
to why we are here.

We are more than
play things for the immortal.
We are more than
fertilizer for the earth.
We are delicate threads
in a great tapestry
of never-ending
cosmic cyclical life.

We are all
quantumly entangled
with everyone
and everything else
that ever was and will be,
and we have been
since our universe
lit up the dark.

What I do unto you,
will eventually traverse
the cosmic strings
and be visited back upon me,
in this life or the next.

Make of Me What I Am

I am the storm and the rain,
the lightning and the thunder.
I am the wind and its havoc,
the hurricane and the swells.

I am the moon and its tidals,
the waves and the wreckage.
I am the quake and the flood,
the wrath and the rubble.

I am the cause
and the result
of all that shall be
and has been before.

I am the fire and the ash,
the drought and the death.
I am the living and the flock,
the dead and their shepherd.

I am the break and the bruise,
the sickness and the fever.
I am the slice and the scar,
the plague and the cure.

I am the seed and the sycamore,
the roots and the forest.
I am the river and the canyon,
the avalanche and the glade.

I am all that was,
all that is,
and I am all that shall be.

I am both without
and within.
I am all you make of me.

Thoughts While Buried

I'm too tired to let go
Too dull to know how
I'm too deep to surface
Too full to breathe now

I'm too dead to dig out
Too dark to even try
I'm too drawn to pull away
Too drained to even cry

The Broken

We are right
and we are wrong.
We are lost
and we are found.

We are human,
stained and cracked.
And we are perfect.

We are dark,
midnight and shadows.
But we are light,
sparks and flames.

We are human,
imperfectly forged.

We are the broken ones
and we are beloved.

Penance

I feel you in my hands
as I sew the sins
of the past.

You vibrate in my bones
as I reap the labors
of the present.

You swim through my veins
as I bloodlet them
of my addiction.

Still, I know you in my depths
as I straddle the crossroads
before me.

This cursed repetition
is my penance.
Shall you be
my salvation?

Savage Soul

I can make peace with silence
and make love with thunder.

I'm a man of quiet reflection,
but I greet walls with fury.

Born of renaissance,
possessed by the ancients.

Unbound by common fear
or mortal sins of the soul.

I am no foe of evolution,
nor do I fear the calm sea.

I embrace the turbulent waters
and the chaos they birth.

I let the swells consume me
and spit me out anew.

I do not tremble in the blackest night,
nor burn in the flames of day.

I carry the shame of the fallen
and the glory of those who rise again.

I have finally become
what the past has made me -

a savage soul
with gentle hands.

Savage Owl Press

Sun and Sky by Kindred
Cover by Kindred
Published by Savage Owl Press
Dallas, TX

© 2018 Kindred
All rights reserved. No portion of this book may be reproduced in any form without permission from the publisher, except as permitted by U.S. copyright law. For permissions contact: permissions@savageowlpress.com

SavageOwlPress.com
@kindred.author on instagram

ISBN-13: 978-1732054905
ISBN-10: 1732054908

www.ingramcontent.com/pod-product-compliance
Lightning Source LLC
Chambersburg PA
CBHW071517040426
42444CB00008B/1679